How to Be a Powerhouse Partner

From "Me" to "We" for a Happier Home

COPYRIGHT

CATALOG

Part 1

Building a Strong Foundation

Chapter 1

Changing How You Think About Partnership

From "Better Wife" to "Powerhouse Partner"

Starting off:

This chapter challenges the outdated idea of a "better wife" and introduces the empowering idea of a "powerhouse partner." We'll stop focusing on how to make your wife better and instead talk about how to build a partnership based on respect, good communication, and common goals. This method makes each person happier, the relationship stronger, and the home a better place for everyone.

Getting rid of the old ideal:

The idea of a "better wife" usually means that one person is more powerful than the other in the relationship. It means the wife has to keep getting better to meet some outside standard, and she often forgets about her own wants and needs. This situation can lead to anger and make it hard to get close.

The Powerhouse Partner's Rise:

If someone actively helps the relationship work, they are a strong partner. They are good at talking about what they need and listening to what their partner has to say. They value their partner's strengths and points of view, which makes room for improvement in both of them. Powerhouse partners are also good at working together and share the duties of running a home and raising children, if they have any.

Powerhouse partnerships have these pros:

There are many good reasons to use the "powerhouse partner" method. First, it helps people be happy with their lives. Both partners feel free to follow their dreams and interests because they put personal growth and open communication first. Second, it makes the bond stronger. Respect, trust, and making decisions together are all things that make a relationship stronger and last longer. Lastly, a strong relationship makes the home a better place to be. Kids do better when their parents work together and communicate and work together in a healthy way.

Changing Your Attention:

It takes conscious effort to change from a "me" attitude to a "we" mentality. To get you started, here are some ideas:

Figure Out What You Both Value: Take some time to think about what's important to you as individuals and as a pair. Knowing your core values can help you set shared goals and make choices together in the future.

Rewriting the Story: Question what you think you know about the roles of men and women in a relationship. Look into tools that help partnerships stay healthy and balanced.

Visualizing Your Ideal partnership: Be honest with your partner about what you want from your partnership. Make a vision board together or think of ways to help each other reach their personal and business goals.

In conclusion:

Adopting the "powerhouse partner" strategy is a process, not a goal. The first step on that road is in this chapter. Working together, talking to each other, and having the same goals can help you build a strong friendship that is good for the whole family. As you go forward, keep in mind that a powerhouse relationship isn't about getting "better"; it's about working together to make your life better and more enjoyable for both of you.

Chapter 2
Knowing Your Love Languages
How to Talk to Your Partner More Effectively

Starting off:

Have you ever felt like you and your partner were talking different languages? You show your partner love in a certain way, but they don't seem to notice. This chapter talks about the idea of "love languages," which can help you and your partner figure out the best way to give and accept love. You can communicate better and feel closer to each other if you learn each other's love languages.

Five Ways to Show Love:

The Five Love Languages, which were created by Dr. Gary Chapman, say that each person has a main way they like to feel and show love:

Words of Affirmation: People who speak this language want to hear words of love, respect, and support.

Compliments, thanks, and affectionate words are all wonderful to them.

Quality Time: For these people, the most important things are undivided attention and meaningful shared events. Put away the things that are distracting you, start talking, and make experiences that will last a lifetime.

Acts of Service: For this love language, actions speak louder than words. Helping your partner out with jobs, errands, or anything else that makes their life easier shows that you love and care for them.

Getting Gifts: This isn't about being materialistic. Giving meaningful gifts, no matter how big or small, is a real way to show your love and show that you've been thinking about what they want.

Physical Touch: For this love language, you need to be close to each other physically, like holding hands, cuddling, or showing care. Having it makes you feel safe and connected.

How to Figure Out Your Love Language:

Think about the questions below to figure out what your main love language is:

✧ What makes you feel loved and cared for the most?

✧ What do you most often complain about in your relationship? (The answer could show a love language that hasn't been used enough)

✧ How do you easily show love to other people?

How to Read Your Partner's Love Language:

Free speech is very important. Here are some ways to find out what language your partner speaks of love:

Tell Them Straight Out: Have a deep talk with them about what makes them feel loved and valued.

Watch What They Do: What kinds of movements seem to make them the happiest? Pay attention to what they complain about most and what they say they like about it.

Watch How They Show Love: What are some normal ways they show love? Do they often tell you nice things, offer to help you with work, or touch you?

Speaking the same language:

At this point, you should know each other's love languages and start using them. How to do it:

Change the way you say things: use their words! If your partner likes positive words, tell them you love them and give them lots of praise. If they like acts of kindness, do them a favor by doing a job they hate.

Be Intentional: There are more than just automatic ways to show love. Spend time and thought on how to show your love in a way that hits home with your partner.

It's important to show appreciation for your partner's attempts to speak your love language, even if they don't always get it right.

More Than the Basics:

There are five main love languages, but some people may value more than one. The important thing is to keep talking and change how you talk over time. Love languages can also change as you and your partner go through different times of your life. Be willing to learn and grow with other people.

How we talk to each other goes both ways:

Knowing the love languages is only one part of being able to talk to someone. It's just as important to listen actively, make your wants clear, and show empathy. Keep in mind that talking to someone goes both ways. Be ready to accept your partner's love in the language they use, even if it's not your first language.

In conclusion:

Love languages are a great way to figure out what your partner wants and needs emotionally. You can have a deeper bond, better communication, and a more fulfilling relationship if you both try to speak the other person's language. Remember that communication is an ongoing process as you start this path of knowledge. Talk, learn, and

grow together as much as possible.

Chapter 3

Trust and respect are the most important things in a happy home

Starting off:

A strong and healthy friendship is built on trust and respect. They make people feel safe, support open communication, and make a space where both people can do well. This chapter talks about how important these foundations are and gives you tips on how to build and keep them in your relationship.

How Trust Works:

When you trust someone, you believe that they will be honest and look out for your best interests. Being open and honest about who you are lets you connect with someone more deeply. This is why friendship is so important:

Security and Stability: Because you know you can count on your partner, the partnership feels safe and stable.

Open Communication: If you don't trust someone, you can't talk to them freely, and private chats make it harder to get close.

Resolution of Conflicts: Trust makes people more willing to find good ways to disagree.

Trust-Building:

Honesty and Integrity: Always tell the truth in what you say and do. Small lies can slowly break down trust over time. Following Through on Promises: No matter how big or small your word is, keep it. This shows that you can be trusted and boosts confidence.

Open Communication: Be honest about your feelings and thoughts, even if they're hard.

Boundaries: Be aware of and respect your partner's mental and physical limits. This shows that you believe them and makes them feel safe.

Being vulnerable means being honest about who you are, including your skills and weaknesses. Being vulnerable makes the connection stronger and builds trust.

How to Understand Respect:

Respect is more than just putting up with your partner. It means putting their thoughts, wants, and feelings first, even if you don't agree with them. This is how respect looks in real life:

- ✧ Active listening means paying attention to what your partner says and how they say it. Don't talk over them or dismiss what they're saying.

- ✧ **Validation:** Let them know that you understand their feelings and situations. Tell them that how they feel is important.

- ✧ **Positive Regard:** Like your partner just the way they are, flaws and all.

- ✧ Be ready to find solutions that work for both of you that are in the middle of what your partner wants.

Building up respect:

Words of Affirmation: Tell your partner how much you appreciate what they bring to the relationship on a regular basis.

Quality Time: Make time to connect with your partner without any other things going on.

Acts of Service: Help your partner out by doing things. This shows that you care about them and want the best for them.

Respectful Disagreements: Learn how to disagree in a way that doesn't involve blaming or attacking others.

A Never-Ending Journey of Trust and Respect:

It takes time and constant work to build trust and respect. There will be bumps in the road, but you can make it a safe place for trust and respect to grow by talking to each other honestly, taking responsibility for your actions, and putting each other's needs first.

Why a partnership based on trust and respect is good:

More Intimate Connection: Being honest and open can help you form a real bond.

Better Resolution of Disagreements: You can handle disagreements better and come up with answers that work for both of you.

More happiness and safety: You can make your relationship safe and supportive so that both parties feel loved and valued.

In conclusion:

By putting trust and respect first, you build a friendship that will last. Don't forget that these cornerstones are not the end goal; they are the beginning of a path. Keep talking to each other, working together, and growing as a group. Your ideas about trust and respect will change as your relationship does. Enjoy the journey that comes with a strong and satisfying relationship.

Chapter 4
The Power of Shared Vision
Getting Your Dreams and Goals to Match

Starting off:

Think about a group of people who are all working toward the same goal. That's the power of having the same goals in a relationship. This chapter talks about why it's important to make sure your goals and dreams are in line with each other and how working together can make your relationship stronger and your life together more enjoyable.

Shared Vision Is Important:

Working together to reach common goals gives people a sense of unity and purpose. As the journey goes on, you become a team and help and support each other.

Drive and Concentration: Having the same goals keeps you both going. Knowing that your partner is on board can help you get through tough times and keep going.

Aligning Values: Creating a shared vision helps you understand your own values and find places where you and the other person can work together. This helps you understand each other better and makes your relationship stronger.

Coming up with a shared vision:

Individual Reflection: Think about your own hopes and dreams for a while. Think about what you want your career, finances, family, hobbies, and overall way of life to be like in the long run.

Open Communication: Talk to your partner about their hopes and dreams in a deep way. Actively listen and ask questions to fully understand their point of view.

Finding Common Ground: Look for places where your goals are similar. Do both of you want to see the world? Putting together a family? Getting into business together? Finding things that everyone has in common is the first step to making a shared goal.

Making a Group Plan: Talk about how you can help each other reach their own goals and work together to reach your common goals. Be honest, adaptable, and willing to make deals.

Seeing Your Future: Make a vision board with someone. Include pictures, words, and quotes that show how your dreams and goals are alike. This picture will help you stay focused and inspired.

How Being Flexible Can Help You:

Life throws curveballs at us. Be ready to change your vision if your interests or circumstances do. To get through these changes together, you need to be able to talk to each other freely and be willing to negotiate.

Benefits Beyond Having the Same Goals:

More Intimate Connection: Working together toward a shared goal makes people feel closer.

More Open Communication: You'll easily talk to each other more honestly and share your hopes, fears, and dreams.

Problem-Solving Skills: Working through problems with others makes your problem-solving skills stronger and gets you ready for the tasks you'll face in life.

In conclusion:

Making a shared goal is not a one-time thing that happens. It shows how much you want to grow together and help each other reach their goals. When your goals and aims are in line with each other, you set the stage for a more satisfying and meaningful relationship. Don't forget that getting to a shared goal is just as important as getting there. Enjoy the process of finding out more about yourself, help each other reach your goals, and enjoy your successes along the way. Along with making your relationship better, this adventure will also help you make a life that is truly satisfying for both of you.

Part 2

Communication & Conflict Resolution

Chapter 5
Learning How to Actively Listen
Really Hearing Your Partner

Starting off:

It can feel like a lost art to really listen to someone in a world full of noise and distractions. But in a relationship, active listening is a key skill for getting closer, understanding, and fixing problems in a healthy way. This chapter talks about the power of active listening and gives you tips on how to become a great listener for your partner.

Besides Just Hearing Words:

Listening actively is a lot more than just hearing what your partner says. It means giving close attention to their words and body language, showing empathy, and trying to figure out how they feel and what they mean by what they say.

Why active listening is good:

That's because when you really listen, you show your person that you care about what they have to say. This makes your relationship stronger and encourages closeness.

Less conflict: Active listening keeps you from misunderstood things and lets you deal with the real problem before it gets worse.

Problem-Solving: You can work together to find answers that work for both of you if you fully understand your partner's point of view.

What Makes Active Listening Work:

Put away things that might take your attention away, like your phone, and turn off the TV. Then look your partner in the eyes.

Be in the Present Moment: Pay attention to what your partner is saying only. Do not think about what you will say or how you will argue against what they say.

Use your body language. Leaning in, nodding, and keeping your stance open all show that you're paying attention and interested.

Ask clarifying questions to try to see things from their point of view. Ask them open-ended questions to get them to say more about how they feel and what they are thinking.

Reflect and Summarize: Rephrase what you've heard every so often to make sure you understand. This shows that you're interested and gives you a chance to ask questions if you need to.

Active listening that goes beyond words:

You should pay attention to your partner's tone of voice, body language, and facial emotions. Often, these visual cues can show feelings that words alone might not be able to show.

Accept Their Feelings: Let them know you understand how they feel, even if you don't agree with them. It can help a lot to say things like "That sounds frustrating" or "I get why you're upset."

How to Stop Bad Listening Habits:

Interrupting: Wait for your partner to finish their thought before you answer.

Giving Advice Without Being Asked: Sometimes all your partner needs is someone to listen, not advice. Only offer answers if they're already looking for them.

Don't play down their feelings or experiences by telling them things like "It's not a big deal" or "You're overreacting."

Taking care of other things at the same time: Doing other things while talking to someone shows that you're not fully interested in what they have to say.

Active listening: a habit that lasts:

Everyone doesn't automatically know how to listen actively. It takes time and skill. As you learn this important skill, be kind to yourself and your partner. Celebrate your wins and use your losses as chances to learn.

Why active listening is good:

If you learn how to actively listen, you can make it easier for people to talk to you, gain their trust and respect, and grow closer to your partner. You'll change your relationship and make your life better together as you start this process of listening to understand.

Chapter 6

Saying What You Want and Need

How to Communicate Well for a Successful Partnership

Starting off:

Clear and honest conversation is key to keeping relationships healthy. But sometimes it can be scary to tell your partner what you need and want. You can make sure your needs are met and your voice is heard in your relationship by using the conversation skills in this chapter.

Why stating needs is important:

Getting rid of frustration: Hiding your wants can make you angry and upset. When you talk to your partner openly, they can understand and address your worries.

Stronger Partnership: When you say what you want and need, you open the door to working together to find answers. This makes your bond stronger and encourages you to work together.

Mutual Fulfillment: To have a fulfilling connection, both people must understand what the other person wants. You can make a life that meets both of your needs if you can talk to each other well.

The Power of Saying "I" Things:

Claims about "you" can sound offensive and put your partner on the defensive. Instead, use clear "I" statements to talk about your wants and feelings without pointing the finger at anyone else.

When you don't want to say "You never spend time with me," try "I feel neglected when we don't have quality time together."

Techniques for Effective Communication:

Pick the Right Time and Place: Don't start talking to your partner when they are busy or stressed. Pick a quiet time when both of you can pay attention to the conversation.

Start with Appreciation: Tell your partner something you like about them to start. This makes everyone feel good and supports honest conversation.

Pay attention to the problem, not the person: Go after the problem, not your partner. Pay attention to the actions that bother you and how they make you feel.

Be Specific: It's hard to help people who make general complaints. Give good examples of what you want or need. Give your partner a chance to say what they think by actively listening to their answer.

Focus on Solutions: Come up with ideas for solutions that meet both of your goals as a team. Be ready to give and take. Say "thank you": Tell your partner you appreciate them listening and being ready to work with you.

More Than Words:

There's more to good conversation than just words. Body language, facial expressions, and the tone of your words are also very important.

✧ Keep your eyes on your date. This shows that you're paying attention to what they are saying.

✧ Don't yell, accuse, or be sarcastic. Instead, speak in a quiet and polite way.

✧ Leaning in, keeping your arms loose, and having a relaxed stance are all signs of open body language.

To Create an Environment for Free Speech:

It takes time for open conversation to happen. It's a constant process that needs dedication from both sides.

✧ **Set up regular check-ins:** Set aside time every day, even if it's just 15 minutes, to talk about your day, your needs, and how you feel.

✧ **Active listening:** Give your person your full attention and show that you value what they have to say.

✧ **Set up a safe space:** Make sure that your partner can talk freely and honestly without worrying about being judged or criticized.

In conclusion:

A key skill for a successful relationship is being able to clearly state your needs and wants. Clear communication, using "I" statements, and carefully listening to your partner are all things that will help you and your partner understand each other and meet your needs. Keep in mind that talking to someone goes both ways. You'll be able to connect with each other better, trust each other more, and live a happier life together as you learn these skills.

Chapter 7

How to Handle Conflict Like a Pro: Tools for Healthy Arguments

Starting off:

There will always be disagreements in relationships. That being said, it doesn't have to be bad. This chapter gives you important tools for handling disagreements in a healthy way, helping each other understand, and coming out of a fight stronger as a pair.

Trouble: Not the Enemy

If you deal with disagreements in a healthy way, they can actually help you grow. They can help you see things from each other's points of view, improve the way you talk to each other, and eventually strengthen your relationship.

The Dance That Hurts:

Getting stuck in bad habits of conflict can hurt your relationship. Keep an eye out for these warning signs:

Personal Attacks: Insults, name-calling, and pointing the finger only make things worse.

Stonewalling means stopping communication or refusing to take part in the talk. This doesn't solve the problem.

The Blame Game: Focusing on who is right and who is wrong makes people hostile and makes it harder to solve problems.

The Powerhouse Way to Handle Conflict:

Powerhouse partners treat disagreements with respect, understanding, and a sincere desire to find answers. Here are some tips on how to handle arguments well:

✧ When you disagree with someone, you don't have to start a full-on fight every time. Pick your battles wisely and pay attention to the things that really count.

✧ **Cool Down:** If you're feeling angry or upset, take a moment to calm down before you talk to someone. If you look at it from a calmer place, you can have a more reasonable conversation.

- ✧ Pay attention to the problem, not the person: Go after the problem, not your partner. Use "I" words to focus on specific actions and how they make you feel.

- ✧ Active listening means really hearing what your partner has to say. To make sure you understand, ask additional questions and rewrite what you've heard.

- ✧ **Together, come up with ideas**. Work with others to find answers that meet both of your needs. Be willing to give and take and find shared ground.

- ✧ Think "We" instead of "Me" vs. "You": deal with things as a group moving toward a common goal.

How to Find a Middle Ground:

In every relationship, you need to be able to compromise. It doesn't mean giving up everything you want; it means coming up with a plan that works for both of you. Be flexible, but don't give up on what you believe in.

Why it's Important to Take Responsibility:

Take responsibility for what you say and do. Take responsibility for your part in the argument and be ready to say sorry if needed.

Moving On:

Celebrate the Resolution: Once you've found a way to get along again, take a moment to appreciate how hard you both worked to make it happen.

Learn from the Mistake: Think about the argument and figure out how you could communicate better next time.

Getting along with others is a skill:

Not everyone is good at handling disagreement in a healthy way. You need to work at it and be ready to learn from your mistakes. It's important not to give up when things go wrong. Enjoy your wins and keep trying to improve the way you talk to people.

The Good Things About Healthy Conflict Resolution:

You can make your relationship better by learning how to handle disagreements in a healthy way. How to do it:

Deeper Understanding: When people talk and listen to each other well, they can better understand each other's wants and points of view.

Stronger Bond: Concluding arguments as a couple builds trust and makes your relationship stronger.

Problem-Solving Skills: Learning how to handle conflicts in a healthy way will help you deal with problems in the future better.

In conclusion:

There will always be disagreements in a friendship. You can make your partnership more satisfying by turning arguments into chances to grow by giving each other the right tools and working together. Remember that talking is very important. You can handle disagreements like a pro and come out better together if you focus on solutions, listen carefully, and

approach conflict with respect and understanding.

Chapter 8

When you forgive someone, you can let go and move on with your life

Starting off:

When you hold on to anger after a fight or betrayal, it can hurt your relationship. Even though it's hard, forgiveness is a powerful way to let go of bad feelings, help people heal, and improve your relationship. This chapter talks about why forgiveness is important and gives you ways to forgive your partner and move on with your life.

How to Understand Forgiveness:

It's not okay to condone your partner's actions or act like the hurt never happened when you forgive them. You have to choose to let go of anger, resentment, and the need for payback. It makes you feel better and helps you think more clearly as you go on.

Why forgiving someone is good:

Stress and anger are reduced: staying angry is bad for your mental health. Forgiving someone lets you let go of bad feelings and find peace within yourself.

Better Relationship: Forgiving helps people heal and lets them trust and be close again.

Personal Growth: Forgiving someone teaches them important lessons about being kind, understanding, and letting go.

The Path to Forgiveness:

✧ Forgiveness doesn't always happen in a straight line. Getting through tough feelings can take time, patience, and a desire to do so. To help you on your way, here are some steps:

✧ **Accept Your Pain:** Don't downplay your pain. Let yourself feel the feelings that come with being hurt.

✧ Try to see things from your partner's point of view, but don't say that you agree with what they did. This doesn't mean you should excuse their behavior, but it can help you understand how they feel.

✧ **Talk About Your Needs:** Be honest with your partner about how you feel and what you need from them to start healing.

✧ **Choose to Forgive (Yourself):** Forgiveness is a gift you give yourself in the end. Getting rid of it lets you move on.

✧ **Set Limits, If Necessary:** Forgiving someone doesn't mean you forget or accept them without question. If you need to, set limits to keep yourself safe from getting hurt again.

Don't forget that you can choose to forgive:

You do not have to forgive your partner. Take some time to heal if you're not ready. But think about how forgiving someone might help your own health and the health of your connection.

Looking for Help:

✧ If it's hard for you to accept your partner, you might want to talk to a therapist or counselor. Their advice and support can help you on your path to healing.

✧ **Moving Forward Together:**

✧ It's possible to start over when you forgive someone.

✧ Rebuild Trust: It takes time and steady work to rebuild trust.

✧ **Reaffirm Your Promise:** Say again that you are committed to the relationship and to each other.

✧ **Focus on the Good:** Work on making your relationship better and healthier, enjoy the good times, and get through the tough times together.

In conclusion:

It takes strength and kindness to forgive someone. By accepting its power, you let go of bad feelings, help others heal, and build a foundation for a happier, stronger connection. Don't forget that forgiving someone is a process, not a goal. As you go through the process, be kind to yourself. You'll find that letting go and going forward

together is very freeing.

Part 3

Nurturing Intimacy & Connection

Chapter 9
Keeping the Spark Alive
Romance and Passion Alive Again

Starting off:

That spark you felt at the start of your relationship is very important. But let's be honest: life gets busy and habits set in, and sometimes that spark needs to be sparked again. This chapter goes into detail about how important it is to keep the romance going and gives you tips on how to do that.

Why love is important:

There's more to romance than big moves and fancy meals. To keep the connection alive and remind your partner why you fell in love in the first place, you need to deepen your relationship. This is why putting romance first is so important:

Stronger Bond: Romantic actions show that you love and appreciate each other, which makes your relationship stronger and more emotionally close.

Less Stress: Spending time with each other can help lower stress and make the relationship more enjoyable.

Partner happiness leads to a happier relationship. Romance keeps the spark alive and can make both people happier in the relationship as a whole.

Bringing the Flame Back:

It's good to know that love doesn't have to be hard or cost a lot of money. Here are some ways to get the love flowing again:

Plan Special Dates: Set aside time for date nights, even if it's just a walk in the park with no kids around. Get back in touch and spend time together.

Little Things Can Make a Big Difference: Write your partner a love note, give them a small gift as a surprise, or offer to do a job that they usually do. Small things like these show that you care and keep the spark alive.

Get Physically Close Again: Don't forget about touching each other. Start a relationship, cuddle up on the couch, or plan a romantic night in.

Try New Things Together: Get out of your comfort zone and do some new things with your partner. Learn how to cook, hike, or dance a new dance. Sharing adventures makes memories that last and brings you closer together.

Saying and doing things that show your partner how much you value them on a regular basis is important. Do not assume that they are there.

Prioritize Quality Time: Set aside time every day, even if it's just 15 minutes, to talk to someone without interruption. Don't talk about other things, just connect with each other.

Show Interest in Their Passions: Show interest in the things they like to do for fun. This makes the link stronger and shows that you care.

If you want to feel better, laugh with your friends or family. Play games, watch a funny movie, or talk about funny times in your relationship. Sharing laughter makes your relationship stronger and helps you remember good times.

Romance needs to be kept alive all the time:

To keep the spark living, remember that it's an ongoing process, not a one-time fix. Here are some more helpful hints:

✧ **Be creative:** Make your love actions fit what your partner wants. What makes them feel liked and loved?

✧ **Talk About Your wants:** Be honest about your wants for romance and closeness. What do you want the relationship to have more of?

✧ **Don't be rigid;** life will throw you curveballs. If you need to, be open and change your plans. Spending good time together is the most important thing.

✧ **Mark Important Occasions:** Don't forget to enjoy birthdays, anniversaries, and other important events. Honor your journey together and tell them you love them.

✧ **In conclusion:**

✧ If you put romance first and work at your relationship, you can keep the spark alive, grow closer, and create a long-lasting and satisfying union. Don't forget that little things can make a big difference. Keep the love alive, put each other first, and enjoy the process of getting your relationship excited again.

Chapter 10
The Quality Time Revolution
Making Time for Connection a Priority

Starting off:

In today's busy world, it's easy to forget to spend important time with our partners. But if you want your relationship to be healthy, you have to make time to meet every day. This chapter talks about how important quality time is and gives you ideas on how to change the way you connect with your partner so that you can build a stronger bond and a happier relationship.

The Importance of Quality Time:

Being in the same room isn't enough to make time quality. It's about giving your partner your full attention, getting closer, and sharing events that make your bond stronger. This is why putting quality time first is important:

Strengthens Your Bond: Making time to connect with each other helps you grow closer emotionally and strengthens your bond.

Quality time makes it easier for people to talk to each other and gives them a safe place to share their thoughts, feelings, and dreams.

Take a break from your daily routines and spend time with each other again. This will help you both relax and feel calm in your relationship.

Brings Back the Spark: Spending quality time together can bring back the beauty and closeness in your relationship.

The Rise of Quality Time:

Move Past Quantity: It's not how many hours you spend together that matters, but how well you talk to each other. Leave all other things behind, be fully present, and focus on bonding with your partner.

Change how you do things: Quality time doesn't have to look the same for every pair. Figure out what you and your partner can do together. Do you like having deep talks, going on exciting trips, or just relaxing on the couch?

Set aside time for quality time: treat it like an important meeting. Make plans for time and try to stick to them as much as possible.

Allow yourself to be unplugged: put away your phones, computers, and other things that might distract you. Really listen to what your partner has to say and give them your full attention.

Plan Things to Do Together: Make plans for things you both like, like trying a new place, going on a hike, or going on a weekend trip. Sharing adventures makes memories that last and brings you closer together.

Accept spontaneity: Allow for unplanned times of connecting. Randomly go for a walk in the park, hold a dance party in the kitchen, or plan a picnic outside for your partner.

Quality Time Aside from Big Events: Big events are great, but don't forget how powerful small, everyday times of connection can be. Something as simple as a cup of coffee in the morning, a walk together in the evening, or just sitting on the couch can mean a lot.

The Power of "We" Time:

It's not just romantic nights that count as quality time. Plan tasks that will help you connect with each other as a team. This could mean working on a project around the house together, helping out a cause you both care about, or just eating a meal as a family.

Pros for people besides the couple:

Setting aside time for quality can help not only your relationship but also your health in general. Strong couple bonds make people less stressed, happier, and more able to help each other.

In conclusion:

Making an effort to connect with your partner more often is what a quality time change is all about. You can make your relationship more satisfying by using these tips to get closer, share more experiences, and become more intimate. Remember that spending valuable time together is an investment in your happiness now and in the future. Make it a point to care for your relationship, and you'll see your love story grow.

Chapter 11

Making Memories That Will Last: Building a Life Together Full of Fun and Adventure

Starting off:

Life is more than just work, bills, and habits. Shared memories, laughter, and a little adventure are all great ways to make a relationship work. This part goes into detail about how important it is to have fun and explore life together and gives you ideas on how to make memories that will last and keep the spark alive.

The Power of Talking About Past Events:

✧ Sharing events brings you closer together, makes you remember good times, and gets your relationship excited. It's important to include fun and excitement in your life together because:

✧ Building a strong bond with your partner by working together to complete a difficult walk or plan a surprise trip makes your relationship stronger and encourages teamwork.

✧ Laughter really is the best medicine. When two people laugh together, it lowers stress, raises happiness, and makes the relationship feel joyful.

✧ **New Views:** When you try new things with your partner, you both learn new things and see each other in a new way.

✧ **Memories That Last:** The things you do together will become treasured memories that you will enjoy remembering for a long time.

How to Find Your Adventure:

Exploring doesn't need to cost a lot of money or be very dangerous. The key is to find things to do that make both of you happy and make you feel connected. Here are some ideas to help you begin:

✧ **Enjoy nature:** go on a walk, check out a new park, have a picnic by the lake, or camp out under the stars.

- ✧ **Try New Things:** Learn how to cook together, dance a new dance, look at the stars, or go to a place you've never been to before.

- ✧ Enjoy local events: go to a concert, a game, a food fair, or an art show in your area.

- ✧ **Plan Big and Small Adventures:** From weekend trips to exploring a new neighborhood, make memories-making activities a top priority.

- ✧ Travel with your partner, even if it's just for a staycation. Traveling opens your eyes to new things and lets you make experiences that will last a lifetime. Plan your ideal trip, check out a nearby city, or just enjoy a fun-filled staycation with different things to do.

- ✧ **Bring back old interests:** Find old hobbies that you and your partner used to enjoy or look for new ones that you both like.

- ✧ **Embrace spontaneity:** Make time for activities that didn't go as planned. Go on a scenic side trip, check out a secret laneway, or decide on the spot to try a new place.

- ✧ **Fun Should Be Part of Everyday Life:** Look for ways to add fun to the things you do every day. Make going to the store a game, hold dance parties in the kitchen, or make movie nights a fun event.

It's Important to Find Balance:

It's important to put fun and excitement first, but don't forget how important balance is. Also, make sure you set aside time to relax, connect with others in silence, and take care of your own needs.

The Adventure Continues:

Making a fun and exciting life is a journey that never ends. To keep the energy going, here are some more ideas:

Be Open to New Ideas: Listen to what your partner has to say and be ready to try new things, even if they aren't what you normally do.

Talk About Your Needs: Be honest about the kinds of adventures you want to go on, and try to find a mix that works for both of you.

Celebrate Your Successes: Remember and enjoy your journeys together, no matter how big or small they are.

Focus on the Journey: Enjoy the process of making memories with your family, not just the end result.

In conclusion:

A relationship that is full of life and fun is a recipe for a happy and healthy relationship. You can make memories that last, improve your relationship, and keep the spark alive by adding shared experiences, laughter, and a bit of excitement to your daily life. Don't forget that life is a journey that should be shared. So, enjoy the trip together, try new things, and write a love story full of laughter, excitement, and moments you'll never forget.

Chapter 12
Being Physically Close
Keeping the Fire Going

Starting off:

An important part of a good romantic relationship is being physically close to each other. It makes you feel close, connected, and emotionally healthy. This chapter talks about why physical intimacy is important and gives you tips on how to build and keep a satisfying physical link throughout your relationship.

Besides the Physical:

There's more to physical closeness than just sex. It includes a lot of different ways to show love and care, such as:

Other Ways of Showing Love: Hugs, kisses, holding hands, and other actions that show love without words build a closeness and an emotional connection.

Emotional intimacy: For physical intimacy to be satisfying, there needs to be a strong emotional bond. To have a healthy physical connection, you need to be able to talk to each other, trust each other, and feel loved and appreciated.

Why being close physically is important:

Strengthens Bond: Being physically close to someone creates hormones that make you feel attached and bonding.

Lessens Stress: Touching someone can lower stress hormones and make you feel calm and healthy.

Boosts Confidence: Being in a satisfying sexual relationship can make both people feel better about their own self-worth and confidence.

Strengthens the Bond: Being physically close to someone can strengthen the mental bond between you two and make you feel closer.

To Keep the Flame Alive:

Being physically close is a process, not a goal. To keep it satisfying over time, both people have to work at it and pay attention to it. Here are some ways to keep your physical bond strong:

Communication is key. Be honest about your wants, needs, and worries about physical closeness.

Prioritize Quality Time: Set aside time to connect in ways that go beyond the body. Plan regular date nights or make time to cuddle and get close emotionally.

Explore Together: Don't be afraid to try new things in the bedroom. Try out different ways to touch, talk, and do things that will bring you closer together.

Take Care of Your Physical and Emotional Health: Looking after your physical and emotional health can help your sexual relationship in a roundabout way.

Celebrate Each Other: Show and tell your partner how much you appreciate them. Tell them you think they're beautiful and desirable.

Embrace spontaneity: Don't let closeness turn into a habit. As a surprise, give each other a massage or do something sweet, or start talking to each other without warning.

Get Professional Help (If You Need It): If you're having trouble with physical closeness, you might want to talk to a sex therapist. They can help you deal with certain problems by giving you advice and support.

Remember that love goes both ways:

Physical closeness should be something that both people enjoy. Focus on telling your partner what you need, respecting their boundaries, and making a safe place for them to explore and talk freely.

Getting close physically over time:

Over time, physical closeness may develop on its own. This is normal and doesn't always mean there is a problem. At every stage of your relationship, you should keep the lines of communication open, make time for quality time together a priority, and be open to new ways to keep the spark alive.

In conclusion:

Being close to each other physically is an important part of a good and happy relationship. You can have a satisfying physical relationship that strengthens your bond and grows your love for each other by putting communication first, fostering emotional connection, and being open to exploring. Remember that getting close physically is a trip that you should both enjoy. Enjoy the trip, put your connection first, and keep the flame alive.

Part 4

Cultivating a Happier Home

Chapter 13

Working together to make the dream come true: splitting up household duties

Starting off:

A happy home life is important for a relationship to work. But doing jobs around the house can often turn into a source of stress and anger. This chapter talks about how important it is to share home duties fairly and evenly, and it gives you ideas on how to make a system that works for both of you.

What It Means to Have Unequal Distribution:

Doing jobs around the house unequally can make people angry, frustrated, and feel like they're being taken advantage of. Setting up a method that both partners agree is fair and equal is important.

What Teamwork Can Do for You:

When you do jobs around the house together, you build a sense of partnership, lower your stress, and get your living space cleaner and more organized.

How to Get Your Fair Share:

There is no one-size-fits-all answer. The best way to do something relies on your specific needs, schedule, and preferences. Take a look at these strategies:

- The 50/50 Split: In this traditional method, chores are split evenly between two people. It's fair, but it might not work if one couple works longer hours or is less physically fit.

- **Use Your Strengths:** Give yourself tasks based on what you're good at and what you like. Does one partner like to cook and the other likes to clean? Use these skills to divide up the work more efficiently.

- Instead of focusing on specific tasks, divide jobs based on how much time each person has to spend on them. This makes sure that each person puts in the same amount of work.

✧ **The Rotating Schedule:** Switch up the jobs once a week or once a month to keep things interesting and make sure that both partners are doing different things.

✧ **Open Communication is Key:** Be honest and open about your needs and tasks. You should be ready to give in and find a way to get along that works for both of you.

Making a Vision Everyone Can See:

Figure Out What's Important: Talk about what a clean and well-organized home means to each of you. Do you care more about having a clean home or having a home-cooked meal every night?

Set Expectations: Make sure everyone knows what you expect from each job. Talk about what "clean" means in your situation and how often certain jobs need to be done.

Be flexible, because life will throw you curveballs. Be ready to change your method when you need to. Each partner can help out if the other is busy one week or the other way around.

Beyond Housework: Emotional Work

There are more duties than just doing jobs around the house.
Think about the mental work that goes into running a home,
like planning, grocery shopping, and making appointments.
Make sure that both partners do their fair share of this
mental work.

The Power of Being Thankful:

Don't forget how much each other has helped. Thank your
partner for their hard work and let them know how
important they are to keeping the house cozy.

In conclusion:

To share household duties well, you need to be able to work
together, talk to each other, and be ready to compromise.
You can lower your stress, make your relationship stronger,
and have a more peaceful home life if you work together to
make a system that feels fair. Everyone in the family needs
to work together to keep the house clean and organized. Use
the power of working together to make a plan that works for

both of you. This will let you focus on what's important: spending time together and building a loving, happy relationship.

Chapter 14

The Art of Appreciation

How to Thank Your Partner for Their Work and Make Them Feel Special

Starting off:

It's easy to forget about the things our partners do in the midst of our busy lives. But showing gratitude is an important part of a healthy friendship. This chapter talks about the power of praise and gives you ideas for how to thank your partner for all of their hard work, no matter how big or small.

How "Thank You" Can Help:

A simple "thank you" can mean a lot. Thanks telling your partner that you see how hard they work, value what they bring to the table, and value having them in your life. Why it's important to show appreciation:

✧ **Strengthens Bond:** When you feel appreciated, your mental bond gets stronger and you start to respect and care for each other more.

✧ **It can make both people happier:** showing and receiving appreciation can make both people happier and improve their general health and happiness in a relationship.

✧ Rewarding your partner for their efforts makes them more likely to keep doing what they're doing, which creates a good cycle in the relationship.

The Love Languages: More Than Words

People express gratitude in different ways, which are called "love languages." Figuring out your partner's love language lets you show your gratitude in a way that has the most impact. There are five main ways to show love.

Words of Affirmation: When it comes to some people, saying nice things about them verbally means the most.

Acts of Service: Some people feel loved when their partner helps them out with chores or jobs.

Receiving Gifts: Some partners like receiving physical signs of love and respect, even if it's not about material things.

Time Together: For some, spending focused, unbroken time together is the most important way to show appreciation.

Touch: Hugs, kisses, and holding hands are all forms of physical love that can be a powerful way to show your partner how much you care.

Making it a habit to be grateful:

How can you show thanks every day? Here are some ideas:

Say what you appreciate: Tell your partner you appreciate specific things they do, no matter how big or small. "Thank you for taking out the trash" or even "I really appreciate you making dinner tonight" help a lot.

Write a Love Note: Put a love note telling them how much you appreciate them somewhere they won't expect to find it.

Give your partner words of support: Tell them you believe in them and that you back their goals and dreams.

Do something small that makes a big difference, like a job they usually ask you to do or surprising them with their favorite coffee.

Enjoy Milestones: Don't forget to honor and enjoy birthdays, anniversaries, and other important dates.

Active listening means really hearing what they have to say and being interested in their day, thoughts, and feelings.

Thank You Beyond Words:

It's not enough to just say "thank you." To show you care without words, try these:

Make eye contact and pay attention to them completely when they talk.

Give them a hug or kiss. Touching someone can be a strong way to show you care.

Leave your phone at home. When you're with someone, pay attention and don't do anything else.

If someone needs help, don't wait for them to ask. Simplify their life on your own.

The Journey of Appreciation:

It takes work and consistency to make showing gratitude a habit. Here are some more helpful hints:

Find Out Their Love Language: Ask your partner what their love language is, and then make your efforts to show your appreciation fit that language.

Be Specific: It's nice to say nice things about someone, but it's even more powerful to say nice things about their deeds or qualities.

Be Sincere: Your thanks should come from the heart. Compliments that aren't true can backfire.

It works both ways, and both people should feel valued. Appreciation should be a normal part of your friendship.

In conclusion:

Appreciation is a strong skill that can help you keep your relationship healthy and happy. By appreciating and celebrating your partner's efforts, no matter how small, you improve your relationship, make them happier, and create a good space where both of you can grow. Thanks are like a gift that keeps on giving. Regularly show your thanks, speak their love language, and watch your relationship grow with each sincere thank you.

Chapter 15: Getting kids to talk to you openly: Making the family stronger

Starting off:

Talking to each other is an important part of any good relationship, including the one between a parent and a child. Talking to your kids in an open and honest way builds trust, makes the family stronger, and gives them the tools they need to deal with the problems of life. This chapter talks about why open communication is important and gives you ideas on how to make your home a safe place for your kids to talk easily.

Why it's important to communicate openly:

Stronger Bond: A parent and child can feel closer and trust each other when they can talk to each other freely.

Well-being emotionally: Kids who can talk about how they feel are better able to handle stress and get through tough situations.

Problem-Solving Skills: Children learn important life skills when they can talk to each other and work together to solve problems.

Positive Self-Esteem: Kids feel good about themselves and confident when they know they are being heard and understood.

Setting up a safe place for honest conversation:

To make a safe space for your kids to talk freely, here are some important things you can do:

✧ Listening actively means giving your kids your full attention when they talk. Put away your other things, look the person in the eye, and listen to really understand.

✧ **Avoid Judgment:** Make sure your kids have a safe place to talk about their feelings without worrying about being criticized or punished.

✧ **Validate Their Feelings:** Let them know that you understand and agree with their feelings, even if you don't agree with them. Let them know that you understand how they feel.

✧ Use "I" Statements: Instead of making accusations, say "I" statements to show how you feel. Because "I feel worried when you..." is better than "You always..."

✧ Wait: It takes time to build trust and honest conversation. Be patient and steady in how you do things.

Open Communication During Childhood:

The way you talk to your kids changes as they get older. For each age group, here are some tips:

✧ In the early years, you should focus on making sure your kids feel safe and loved so they can talk and show their feelings without words.

✧ When you reach school age, conversations get more complicated. Get them to talk about their day, their friends, and how they're feeling.

✧ **Teenagers:** Teenagers want to be on their own, but they also need help. Give them a safe place to talk about tough topics like group pressure, relationships, and problems in school.

People can talk to each other in two ways:

Talking to each other freely goes both ways. Here's how to make sure you communicate well:

Start a Conversation: Talk to your kids often, even if it's just about something boring. We can still talk to each other this way.

Be Approachable: Make yourself open and easy to get in touch with. Tell your kids that you'll always be there for them to talk to.

Allow Them To Have Privacy: Your kids will need to be alone sometimes. Respect their boundaries and keep the lines of conversation open.

The Good Things About Open Communication:

By encouraging open conversation, you build a strong base for a healthy family. Here are some more advantages:

Less Conflict: Early detection and resolution of problems are made easier by open communication.

Better Decisions: Kids are more likely to take part in making choices when they feel heard, which leads to better results.

Good Decisions for Life: Kids can make good decisions and stay away from dangerous actions when they can talk to each other freely.

In conclusion:

Getting your kids to talk to you freely is an ongoing process, but the benefits are huge. You can strengthen your family's bond, improve their mental health, and give them the tools they need to succeed in life by making sure they have a safe place to talk, listen, and express themselves. Remember that talking to people is a gift. As a family, keep the lines of communication open and watch as everyone does well.

Chapter 16

Getting Through Life's Storms

Helping Each Other Through Hard Times

Starting off:

Life has many changes and twists that you don't expect. It's likely that people will get sick, lose their jobs, have money problems, and face other problems. This chapter talks about how important it is to be there for each other during life's storms and gives you ways to get through hard times as a strong, united team.

The Power of Working Together:

Having a good partnership is very helpful when things are hard. When life gets tough, it can make a huge difference to know that your partner is there for you, supporting and encouraging you.

Problems as chances to get better:

Challenges can be hard, but they can also be chances to grow. They can make your relationship stronger, help you understand each other better, and give you a new sense of power when you face them together.

Helping your partner through tough times:

Here are some ways you can be a good partner during hard times:

Listen: Give your partner a safe place to talk about their feelings, fears, and complaints without fear of being judged. Say something positive to your partner. Have faith in their ability to get through this. Say nice things about them and remind them of their skills.

Offer Real Help: Doing chores around the house, running errands, or taking care of children can make them feel better and give you mental space.

Respect Their Needs: Some people need room to work through their problems, while others want to be touched. Pay attention to what your partner wants and accept how they deal with things.

Keep the lines of communication open: Be honest and open about what's going on. Tell them about your worries and offer your support in a way that makes them feel good.

Think about the team: Don't forget that you're all in this together. Say things like "we" and stress that you'll handle the problems as a group.

Celebrate Small Wins: Don't forget to celebrate even the smallest wins along the way. This keeps you motivated and gives you a feeling of progress.

Take Care: If your cup is empty, you can't pour from it. Make sure you take care of yourself first so you can be a good help for your partner.

Don't forget that you're not alone:

Don't be afraid to ask for more help. Depending on the problem, you might want to think about therapy, support groups, or cash counseling.

Coming Out Stronger:

When you help each other through tough times, you improve your relationship, become more resilient, and value your partnership even more. How to do it:

Deeper Understanding: Dealing with problems together helps you learn more about each other's skills, weaknesses, and ways of dealing with things.

Strengthens Your Bond: Facing problems together makes your bond stronger and gives you a sense of "us against the world."

Increased Resilience: Going through hard times with others teaches you important ways to deal with them and makes you stronger for future challenges.

In conclusion:

Life will have storms, but you don't have to go through them by yourself. You can get through tough times as a pair stronger and closer by always being there for each other, talking openly, and putting up a united front. Remember that your relationship is what makes you strong, soothes you, and always backs you up. Help each other out and work through problems together, and your love story will get through anything.

Part 5

The Powerhouse Partner Mindset

Chapter 17
Growing All the Time
Putting Money Into Yourself and Your Relationship

Starting off:

Growth is good for a friendship that is healthy. Like a plant, it needs to be cared for and fed regularly to grow well. This chapter talks about how personal growth and investment in your relationship are important. It also gives you ideas for how to keep your love story alive and changing.

Why it's important to keep growing:

Personal Fulfillment: Putting money into your own growth makes you happier and lets you be your best in a relationship.

Needs That Change: Your wants and needs will change over time, both as people and as a couple. You can adapt and keep your friendship alive by growing all the time.

New Points of View: Getting to know new things and broadening your thoughts keeps the spark alive and gives your relationship new life.

Stronger Partnership: When you help each other grow, you improve your relationship and feel like you have a common goal.

Putting money into yourself:

Follow your interests and hobbies; schedule time for things that make you happy and complete.

Encourage personal growth by giving yourself mental and emotional challenges. You might want to take lessons, read, or go to workshops.

Prioritize your physical and mental health: Take care of your physical and mental health by working out, eating well, learning how to deal with stress, and getting professional help if you need it.

Putting money into your relationship:

✧ **Keep the lines of communication open.** Talk about your wants, needs, and hopes for the future of your relationship on a regular basis.

✧ **Schedule Quality Time:** Even if you're busy, set aside time to connect with others. Try new things, have deep talks, and grow your emotional closeness with each other.

✧ You don't have to stop having date nights. Plan regular date nights, even if it's just a vacation or a picnic in the backyard.

✧ Praise your partner for all they do for you and tell them you appreciate them. Let them know that you value their appearance and the work they've done.

✧ **Take on new challenges:** get out of your comfort zone with a friend. Learn a new skill, go on a trip, or take a class together. Sharing adventures makes your bond stronger and creates memories that last a lifetime.

✧ **Seek Professional Help:** If your relationship is giving you trouble, you might want to talk to a therapist or counselor about it. They can help you figure out how to deal with difficult situations.

Growth that never stops is a journey, not a goal:

You will always be growing, and your relationship will change as time goes on. Here are some more helpful hints:

Accept Change: Things will always change. Let yourself and your partner change and grow as a couple and as people.

Celebrate Each Other's Growth: Cheer each other on as they reach personal and business goals.

Think of problems with a "growth mindset," which means that you believe you can learn and get better together.

In conclusion:

You have to keep putting money into yourself and your relationship, but the benefits are huge. You can create a love story that is alive and changing by putting personal growth first, encouraging open conversation, and embracing new experiences together. Don't forget that growth is a process, not a goal. Enjoy the process, and be proud of each other's accomplishments. Your love story will grow as you both learn and grow together.

Chapter 18
Celebrating Your Uniqueness
How to Make a Strong Relationship While Accepting Differences

Starting off:

A healthy friendship depends on two things: being together and being yourself. A strong bond is important, but healthy couples also value the things that make each other special. This chapter talks about how important it is to value your own uniqueness while building a strong and helpful relationship.

The beauty of being different:

When two people from different backgrounds, experiences, and personalities get together, it makes the connection more interesting and full. Here's why it's important to be yourself:

Personal Growth: You can grow and discover new hobbies when you're with someone who supports your uniqueness.

New Views: Your partner's unique point of view can make you think about things in new ways and help you see things in a bigger picture.

Stronger Bond: When two people in a relationship value and respect each other's differences, it makes them feel safe and accepted.

Building a Bridge Instead of Walls:

Being yourself is important, but having a strong base is still very important. Here are some ways to find peace when there are disagreements:

Shared Values: Even if you don't agree on everything, make sure you share basic values like loyalty, honesty, and respect. These ideals that you both agree on bring you together.

Open Communication: Be honest about your wants, needs, and limits when you talk to others. Honest and respectful conversation is needed to find a balance between doing things together and doing things on your own.

Consensus: In any relationship, it's important to be able to give and take. Help each other follow your dreams and make time for activities and hobbies that you both enjoy.

Love what makes you different: Enjoy and praise your partner's oddities and hobbies, even if they don't match your own.

Keep your own identity: Don't let the connection make you lose who you are. Spend time with friends, do the things you love, and make time for your hobbies.

Accepting Your Uniqueness in Everyday Life:

Individuality can be a part of your daily life in these ways:

Follow Your Own Interests: Tell each other to follow your own hobbies and interests. Taking some "me time" can help you feel better and bring new energy back to your relationship.

Help each other reach their goals; be their supporters. Support your partner's goals and enjoy their successes, even if they're not things you both like.

Maintain Separate Social Circles: Having friends who are not in the same group as you helps you keep your own identity and social links.

Plan Activities for "Alone Time": Make plans to do things by yourself that make you happy, like reading a book, going for a run, or spending time in nature.

Come Back Together with Newfound Appreciation: After focusing on your own hobbies, getting back together makes you value each other and your connection even more.

Being unique does not mean being independent:

Being proud of your uniqueness is important, but it shouldn't make you feel disconnected. To keep your relationship strong, do these things:

✧ **Maintain Intimacy:** Make time for quality time together a priority, stay physically and emotionally close, and take care of your relationship as a team.

✧ **Shared Goals and Dreams:** Talk about your goals and dreams for the future, even if you have different hobbies.

When you work together on something, your bond gets stronger.

✧ Teamwork is key to making dreams come true. Face problems and get through life together. Help each other through good times and bad, even when you're having your own problems.

In conclusion:

A strong relationship values both being together and being unique. Respecting each other's differences, encouraging open conversation, and finding a good balance are all things that will help your relationship grow and be happy. Accept what makes you different, help each other grow, and watch your love story grow as the depth of your individualities come together. Remember that having a strong base lets you be yourself while building a long relationship with someone who will support you.

Chapter 19
The Power of Gratitude
Growing Positivity for a Happy Life Together

Starting off:

Being thankful is a strong feeling that makes relationships stronger and brings happiness. You might forget about some things when you're busy with everyday things. This chapter talks about why thanks is important in a relationship and gives you ways to show your partner and yourself how much you value your life together.

Reasons to be thankful:

Being grateful is more than just saying "thank you." It's consciously noticing and appreciating the good things about your relationship and your partner. This is why being thankful is so important:

Strengthens Bond: Being thankful for your partner shows them you value their presence and what they bring to the relationship. This makes you feel closer to each other and strengthens your emotional bond.

Makes People Happier: Showing and getting gratitude can make both people happier and healthier.

Putting the Focus on the Good: Being thankful changes your attention to the good things about your relationship, which makes you feel better.

Creates a Positive circle: When you show your partner gratitude, they are more likely to do the same for you. This starts a positive circle of appreciation in your relationship.

How to Develop a Thankful Attitude:

Consider adding these ways to be thankful to your daily life: Say what you appreciate: Tell your partner you appreciate specific things they do, no matter how big or small. A thank-you note like "thanks for making dinner" or "thanks for listening" is very helpful.

Write a Gratitude Note: Put a love note telling them how much you appreciate them somewhere they won't expect to find it.

Active listening means paying attention to your partner and genuinely wanting to know about their day, their thoughts, and how they feel.

Express Appreciation for Nonverbal Acts: Thank them for their hard work in ways that go beyond words. Note and thank them for things like taking out the trash or making your coffee in the morning that you don't ask them to.

Celebrate Milestones: Birthdays, anniversaries, and other important events should be remembered and celebrated, no matter how big or small they are.

Thank You More Than Words:

It's not enough to just say "thank you." Here are some things you can do to show your appreciation:

Plan a Special Date Night: Make sure the date night fits your partner's hobbies. This will show that you took the time to show your appreciation.

Do a Chore They Usually Do: To surprise them, do a chore they usually do. This will make their life easier and show you value their hard work.

Offer a massage or help with a project: Small acts of kindness, like touching someone or offering to help them with a project, show that you care and appreciate them.

Making it a habit to be thankful:

Being thankful is an ongoing process, not a one-time thing. To make it a habit, try these things:

Start a gratitude journal and write down things you're thankful for about your partner every day.

Share Gratitude at Dinner: Every time you sit down to eat, say one thing you're thankful for about your partner or your relationship.

Focus on the Good: Even when things are hard, train your mind to think about the good things about your relationship.

Being thankful is a gift

Being thankful is a gift that keeps on giving. By telling your partner how much you appreciate them and your life together, you improve your relationship, make them happier, and create a good, supportive space where both of you can grow.

In conclusion:

A easy but effective way to build a fulfilling and long-lasting relationship is to practice gratitude every day. In case you forgot, praise is a way to show love. Use the power of thanks to make your love story grow. Say it often and from the heart.

Chapter 20
Your Happily Ever After Starts Now
How to Build a Lifetime of Love and Joy

Starting off:

A lot of fairy tales end with "happily ever after," but in real life, a good relationship is more of a journey than a destination. This chapter brings together all the lessons that have been talked about in this book. We celebrate the journey of love here and give you the tools you need to build a happy, long-lasting relationship.

You Can Choose Love, Not Just Feel It:

Even though intense and thrilling feelings at the start are important, conscious choices are what make true love grow. It means you promise to take care of your relationship, help each other grow, and be there for each other through life's storms.

Putting together a Strong Base:

For a friendship to last, it needs to have a strong base. Here are some important bases:

Open Communication: Being able to talk to each other honestly and openly is an important part of any good relationship.

Shared Values: Having differences can be good, but make sure you share core values like loyalty, trust, and respect.

Honor each other: Be kind, respectful, and understanding to each other, even when you differ.

Healthy limits: Set healthy limits to protect your own identities and your mental health in the relationship.

To Keep the Love Alive:

Love changes over time. These tips will help you keep the spark alive as you go through life together:

Make quality time a priority: Even if you're busy, set aside time to meet. Set up regular date nights, talk about important things, and grow your emotional closeness.

Take a chance on new things: get out of your comfort zone together. Go to a new place, take a class, or try something new together. Sharing adventures makes memories that last and brings you closer together.

Praise your partner for all they do for you and tell them you appreciate them. Let them know that you value their appearance and the work they've done.

Maintain Physical Closeness: Being close to each other physically is an important part of a good relationship. Find out what you want and need, and keep up a healthy amount of physical affection.

Don't forget that you're a team:

Think of your friendship as a team. Help each other reach their goals, enjoy each other's wins, and work through problems together.

Enjoy the Journey:

The path of love is full of happiness, fun, hard times, and growth. Accept the good and bad times, learn from each other, and get better as a group.

Happily Ever After is still being written:

Working at the relationship, talking to each other, and being able to change are all important for making it work. There will be bumps in the road, but if you work hard, you can get through them and come out better.

In conclusion:

Now is the start of your happily ever after. By following the ideas in this book, you can set yourself up for a lifetime of love, happiness, and growth. Don't forget that love is a verb. Pick your partner every day, tell them you love them, and work with them to make your love story last. One part at a time, you can write your own happily ever after if you work hard and make a promise to each other.

Bonus

Extra Chapter

Here is a bonus chapter from Powerhouse Partner
A Marriage Life Story

Have you ever thought about what it takes to be a great partner in real life? This extra chapter tells the story of Sarah and Michael, a married couple who have been through the good and bad parts of marriage for over twenty years while living by the principles this book talks about.

In the beginning, building a base

Sarah and Michael became friends in college because they both liked to laugh and try new things. Early on, they made it clear that they could talk to each other about anything, from their hopes and dreams to their financial plans. Even though they were very different (Sarah was a meticulous planner and Michael was a spontaneous free spirit), they learned to deeply accept each other's strengths and weaknesses.

Taking on Problems Together:

Things went wrong in their lives. Sarah's job setback put their communication skills to the test, but Michael's unwavering support and belief in her helped her get through it. Later, Sarah was a rock of strength for Michael's family during a tough time, giving both emotional support and practical help. They dealt with problems as a team through good times and bad. With each problem they solved, their bond grew stronger.

The Power of Being Thankful:

Sarah and Michael always cared about each other. Giving thanks was a big part of their relationship. They did everything from simple "thank yous" for everyday jobs to leaving handwritten love notes on the counter. Sarah often told Michael how much she liked his sense of adventure and planned weekend trips with him to keep the spark alive.

Michael, for his part, liked how organized Sarah was and knew he could always count on her to be calm when things got tough.

Growth that never stops:

Sarah and Michael were both unhappy with things staying the same. Michael started taking classes in carpentry, which was a hobby he had always wanted to try, and Sarah started taking evening classes to follow her lifelong interest in photography. They helped each other grow as people by going to workshops together and praising each other's successes.

Accepting Your Uniqueness:

Sarah and Michael were deeply linked, but they also kept their own identities. Sarah liked going to book clubs with her friends, and Michael played sports in a local league.

They were able to recover and bring new energy to their relationship by doing these "me time" things.

One Chapter at a Time to Happily Ever After:

Sarah and Michael's marriage today shows how strong it can be to work together. They've been through life's storms together and celebrated both big and small wins. As their relationship grows, they laugh together, always be there for each other, and accept each other's uniqueness. They show that "happily ever after" is not a place you get to, but a trip you take together with communication, appreciation, teamwork, and a desire to keep growing.

Lessons from Michael and Sarah:

- Free speech is very important.
- Strong foundations are built on shared ideas.
- A happy relationship is fueled by appreciation.

- Accept and encourage each other's growth.

- Problems can make your bond stronger.

- Every day, you can choose to love again.

The Last Word:

The story of Sarah and Michael is moving. Incorporate the lessons they've learned from their journey into your own relationship, and it will last. Don't forget that the two of you are strong partners who are writing their own love story one piece at a time.